I'm Already Home

Keeping your family close
when you're on TDY

Elaine Gray Dumler

Frankly Speaking
Westminster, Colorado

CB

Published by Frankly Speaking
6460 W. 98th Court, Westminster, CO 80021 • 303-430-0592
Elaine@ElaineDumler.com

CB

Visit www.ImAlreadyHome.com

CB

I'm Already Home – Keeping Your Family Close when You're on TDY
Elaine Gray Dumler
ISBN 0-9740359-0-4

Printed in the United States of America
BA   10 9 8 7 6 5 4 3 2 1
Library of Congress Control Number: 2003094993

About the Cover

The cover photograph is by U.S. Air Force SSgt. Thomas J. Sobczyk, Jr. and is used with permission of both the photographer and the wonderful family portrayed in the picture. Meet the Hoffmanns: Major Pete Hoffmann is from the Wisconsin Air National Guard's 128th Air Refueling Wing, and is embracing his family upon his return from Operation Enduring Freedom on May 1, 2002. Shown in the photo are his wife, Sue Hoffmann and their 12 yr. old twin daughters, Kassey and Trina. Not shown, because she's lovingly engulfed in the middle of the hug, is 10 yr. old Rachel.

Major Pete Hoffmann has recently been deployed, and we invite you to share in the life of this family. You can receive updates about the Hoffmanns at www.ImAlreadyHome.com.

TDY=Temporary Duty away from your permanent Station

Cover design and layout by:
Karen Saunders, MacGraphics
Aurora, Colorado

Edited by:
Denise Hmieleski
P.O. Box 709
Lafayette, CO 80026-0709

Page layout by:
Laura Vincent, BOSS Printing
Broomfield, Colorado

Acknowledgements

I am grateful to many people who helped with this book. Thanks to LeAnne Ahearn, Colorado National Guard Family Readiness Specialist who provided information and proofreading resources. Laura Benjamin, Management Development Consultant/Speaker/Author and seven-year Veteran of the United States Air Force (enlisted), thanks for reading the manuscript for military accuracy and for all your kind words along the way. You always told me I was on the right track. Immense gratitude goes to CPT. Ann Dirks, Colorado National Guard Family Program Coordinator for spending so much time with me in interviews, and for supporting the distribution of the book to families. You helped me to put a "face" on all the military contacts I made.

Thanks to Greg Godek for being there to help with all the questions I had about writing and publishing, especially at the beginning. You didn't *have* to do it; you just did! I'm indebted to Bill Goss for his contacts, information, and support with Military.com. I can never repay Denise Hmieleski for the amazing editing job. You made my words actually sound like I wanted them to!

To the members of my Mastermind groups: Fred Berns, Marguerite Ham, Melly Kinnard, Tom Letourneau, Brad Montgomery, Robert Oxley, Jackie Perrett, LeAnn Thieman and Bob Wendover. You all remained faithful cheerleaders and are more important to me than you know. Thanks to Christine Oxley and Sharon Weinberg for the countless hours of research, verifying, and phone work that you devoted to the project.

My heartfelt gratitude goes to Mike Romero for sharing your soulful and spirited thoughts with me during our interview. I feel gifted to have my readers learn from you. A special thanks goes out to Lisa White, unit volunteer for the Colorado Army National Guard's Family Readiness Center for spending all that time on the phone with me. Your insights and ideas fueled me to expand the book to cover more areas. Special thanks to Julie-ann Goldstein and Tara Ewing for sharing your military families with me and making me feel like I was invited into your living rooms.

Finally, I thank God for planting the original vision of the book in my heart and selecting me to be the messenger for helping to make better families.

Dedication

This book is dedicated to my husband (Larry) and
my son (Bryan) who showed me how rewarding it is
to raise kids. And to my parents (Ralph and Josie),
sisters (Rondi and Nancy), and brother (Brad) where
I learned about love and laughter from
the beginning—even in the tough times.

Bryan, I recognize that the catalyst for this book was
the article you and I wrote about family relationships
for *Professional Speaker* magazine.
Thanks for helping me with that.

Beyond the dedication, this book wouldn't have been
written without the emotional inspiration
that came from my sister (Nancy Early) and
her wonderful family (Jim, Stacy and Kenny).
When Nancy lost her battle with cancer,
her family showed more love and support
than I thought was possible.
They were also an inspiration to many who were
around them during that time.
I love you.

Table of Contents

Introduction 1

Chapter 1 – Ideas for the Pre-deployment Phase
(from 6-8 weeks before deployment) 7

Leaving a Piece of You Behind 9

Picture Perfect 13

You're My Top Priority 15

A Conversation with Lisa White 18

Chapter 2 – Ideas for the Deployment Phase
(during deployment) 25

Thinking of You 26

Because I Understand 29

Spouses...Are You Listening? 32

Let's Get Personal 35

It's a Communication Thing 37

Fun Projects for Getting the Kids Involved 42

More Fun Stuff and Projects 46

Chapter 3 – Post-deployment . . . And Beyond
(getting back on track) 53

Home Remedies: Traditions to Build at Home 56

In My Opinion...Top 10 List of What
Worked for Me and My Family 61

Chapter 4 – Out of the Mouths of
Babes...What the Kids Said 63

Talking with Michael Romero 71

About Family Services Centers 75

Resources & Support List 79

Epilogue 85

In Appreciation 87

Permissions / Footnotes 88

About the Author 89

Also By Elaine Dumler 90

Order Form.................................... 91

"I'm Already There"

He called her on the road
from a lonely, cold hotel room
Just to hear her say *"I love you"* one more time.
And when he heard the sound
of the kids laughing in the background
he had to wipe away a tear from his eye.
A little voice came on the phone
and said *"Daddy, when you coming home?"*
He said the first thing that came to his mind:

"I'm already there.
Take a look around—
I'm the sunshine in your hair,
I'm the shadow on the ground,
I'm the whisper in the wind,
I'm your imaginary friend,
and I know I'm in your prayers.
Oh, I'm already there!"

– Lonestar

Introduction

If you've picked up this book, it's probably because you are personally affected by a military separation. Maybe you are a soldier about to be deployed. You've heard from the Family Readiness Center that you need to stay in touch with your family, and now you want to know how. Or maybe you're a family member of someone who's being deployed or on active duty training. The military doesn't enlist only soldiers; they enlist families. You're looking for ways to lessen the impact of the separation.

That's what this book is about. It's about you. It's about your family. It's about keeping you close when you're apart. Togetherness—it's the heart of the family; it's the heart of your family.

I define a family as a particular group of people who love, care for, and support each other. Family can also be considered a place. It's a place where you should feel safe and cared about even if other family members don't always agree with you. The family is a foundation for your social and emotional growth, financial stability, and education. You carry what you absorb from its teaching as you take your place in society. Families may look very different these days, but they contain the same kind of love.

American families are being challenged by trying times in the current political life of our country. When war or the threat of war begins to infiltrate our nation, we have lots of moms, dads, sons, and daughters in the military waiting for deployment. This causes families to be separated for incredibly long spans of time and by phenomenal distances. Many spouses remain at home

1

to handle the roles previously held by both, and the kids may be left to hear bedtime stories from others for a while.

No matter where we are, we need to remember that distance is just an illusion. When we take the time to stay connected, we can still feel close to someone who's thousands of miles away. If we don't take the time, we can feel distanced from someone who is at the other end of the house.

As someone who has many friends serving in the military, I understand the difficulty of being separated from one's family. I, myself, am a professional woman who travels about a third of the time on business. I'm a mom raising a son who recently went off to college and a stepmom with two grown stepsons. I'm also a long-distance daughter and a sister who cared for a sister living in a transplant house before passing away from cancer at 41. (I'm in awe of how she kept her family connected during this time.)

I didn't grow up in a military family, but I don't think that's a requirement to be able to feel the impact that being in the military has on a family. I was a carefree high school teenager in the late '60s and have only two vivid recollections of the war in Vietnam. The first was when a friend of mine lost her brother; the second was when I watched a group of college fraternity brothers sit in silence in front of the television watching the draft lottery on December 1, 1969. I swear that was the only time I ever saw college kids so quiet. I remember feeling very lucky not to have close family members in the age range to serve.

During the conflict in the Persian Gulf, my own son was only eight. Things are different now. My son is 20, and I realize how close I am to being the mom of someone who could be in the military. Because of the tragic events of September 11, 2001, the United States will always be on alert for the threat of terrorism. We currently have 60,000 troops stationed around the world on assignment to fight terrorism.

The faces of the brave people who serve in our armed forces have changed, too. In the Vietnam War, an overwhelming majority of U.S. service men and women were single. Today, 57% are married, and of those, 46% have children. 73% of those children are 11 years of age or younger. The biggest changes, however, have occurred for women. 14% of the military population are now women, and 20% of these women are in joint service marriages where both spouses are serving.[1]

The Gulf War was the first time that we saw mothers, along with fathers, being deployed. So, in addition to more frequent deployments, family separations are having a greater impact. It's no wonder that in a U.S. Army medical research report, 59% of soldiers stated that the number of deployments had hurt the stability of their marriage and put a strain on their families.[2]

The Department of Defense is working hard to provide support for its military families through its creation of Family Centers all around the world. These centers offer youth programs at a total of 320 locations to serve the 1.3 million children of military families.[3]

Family separations are occurring more frequently than ever before, and that's why this book is so timely. The ideas presented here are simple steps you can take to keep you and your loved ones as connected as possible. You'll see what other people do to bridge the distance, and I'll also be sharing some stories from my own life and family about keeping that strong connection. Some are funny and some are touching; I hope all will be inspiring.

I've conducted interviews, done personal research, and compiled the observations and ideas within these pages. While some strategies are specific to military personnel, others are tailored to the unique demands of the military family. Included are things your family can do before, during, and after deployment. You'll also find a section about traditions that can create a firm family foundation and start you thinking of wonderful new ways to say, "I love you and miss you."

Technology has certainly helped close the gap between us when we're apart, but it doesn't replace the special times, the special moments, and the personal ways you have of sharing time with the family when you're right there with each other. This book will help you take your own special, personal times with you when you're away.

I'm Already Home is designed to help you discover unique and wonderful ways to stay connected when you're apart from each other. It's as simple as that. You may already have a couple of traditions in place but would just like to try something new for a change. By bringing you what other families around the country do, I hope you find at least a few new ideas that spark you to think, "That's cool. We should try that." Take an idea and apply a special twist to it so that *your* family can own it now.

I encourage you to write on the pages, and make personal notes in the margins when something strikes you. Then you'll know where to quickly find that special idea.

My prayer is for every service person's safe return, and I hope that the messages in *I'm Already Home* will play a small part in easing your family through this challenging experience.

Savor your family like you savor a fine wine.
Take the time to truly experience
ALL the benefits they have to offer.
Don't gulp them; just sip slowly.

Chapter 1

Ideas for the Pre-deployment Phase
(from 6 to 8 weeks before deployment)

One of the most difficult challenges for family members of those who are deployed is that our hearts ache for the safety of our loved one. The uncertainty of his/her return is always hanging over our heads, and we just can't seem to let it go.

I was scared when my son, Bryan, got behind the wheel of a car for the first time. I was scared when he went off to college. How could I possibly take care of him? I couldn't. I had to let him go. A friend gave me a verse that helped me through the challenging times of letting my son grow up. This verse has been on my refrigerator since his 16th birthday. Although it's more about "letting go" in the natural course of growing up, I pass it along to you with my wish that it will make your separation easier and help you with some of that worry:

As parents and grandparents, uncles and aunts, one of
the hardest things we may have to do is let go of our

children so that they can learn something new. So whether we are handing over the car keys to a newly licensed driver or taking the training wheels off a bike for a first-grader, we may hesitate or feel unsure that what we are doing is right.

But we do more than let go of the car keys and take off the training wheels to allow the children to experience learning firsthand. We also pray for them, remaining strong and supportive, for we know that God is taking greater care of them than we could ever hope to.

Letting go and letting God be in charge, we are able to relax and enjoy the experience of watching our children— and even adults—discover more about what they are capable of doing and achieving.

Reprinted with permission from *Daily Word*™

A brief reminder: Upon deployment, there is always a shortage of space in terms of what you can take with you. Review the ideas on packing remembrances, and then determine how you might make what you take as compact as possible. For example, in addition to taking wallet-size photos, you might use your computer to scan your favorite photos, reduce them, and print them all on one sheet.

Let's get started on our journey...

Leaving a Piece of You Behind

This first connection idea was contributed by a working mom and her 11-year-old daughter. Eleven is a tough age for any child and can be just as hard on parents when they can't be around as much as they'd like. This was the case in their particular family.

1 Every morning Mom would see Ashley off to school and then follow her out the door on the way to work. Mom worked a long day and often didn't arrive home until 6:00 or 6:30. Ashley would come home after school with all her social crises and just want to know that her mom was available, but the house was empty. Mom also felt a huge void at the end of her workday as she longed to be home so she could listen. *How can I let Ashley know that even when we're not in the same room, we can still feel the touch of each other's hands and heart?* That thought gave way to an idea.

After dinner that evening, Mom got two sheets of copy paper and a set of colorful crayons. Then she parked her daughter at the kitchen table. "We're going to color!" her mom replied to the look of surprise on Ashley's face. Then she instructed Ashley to set her hand flat on the paper, take a crayon and trace around it just like she used to do in kindergarten, and she would do the same thing on her own paper.

When she had done that, Ashley looked up and said, "Ok, now what?"

"Now we're going to color together," replied her mom. "Pick up your favorite colors and have fun coloring in your hand. Be as creative as you'd like. Make it look like 'you,' and I'll do it, too."

So both of them spent 15 minutes completing their works of art. When they were done, they held them next to each other with a glow of personal satisfaction.

Then to Ashley's surprise, her mom said, "Ok, now we switch them! You give me yours and I'll give you mine."

Each drawing was slipped into a plastic page protector to keep it clean, and then exchanged with the following instructions from Ashley's mom: "We each have a small piece of each other. Ashley, you put my picture in one of your notebooks, and I'll hang your picture next to my desk. Whenever you wish that I were there with you to listen or reassure you, open your notebook and place your hand on the drawing of my hand. In that instant, no matter where you are, we'll be together. When I'm at work and get homesick for you, I'll place my hand over yours on the drawing by my desk. I know I'll feel your love and thoughts coming through the drawing. When we have each other's hands, we have each other's hearts. No matter what, we'll always be together."

What a wonderful way to realize that distance is relative. The people you love, and who love you, are the most important people in your life. When children grow up, they'll realize that you weren't always together, but they will remember the creative ways you chose to stay in touch with them while you were gone. Spend some time with the members of your family to create your own *handprints*. When you're thousands of miles apart, just touch the handprints and you'll be transported home in your mind.

2 Let's ask a serious question: Can you sing? Even if you don't have a voice like Frank Sinatra or Whitney Houston, your kids will love hearing it. Record a "sing-along" tape or CD for the kids to play in the car. They can sing their favorite songs along with you, or they can just listen to their favorite recording artist—YOU!

3 Do you have favorite stories that you like to read to your children at bedtime? They don't have to miss out on hearing them. Videotape yourself reading bedtime stories for your children. They can play the tape and read along with you. Do you have a new baby? Videotape yourself singing lullabies.

4 Have your soldier put his or her picture on a coffee mug for each member of the family. Then you can all have morning coffee (or juice) together.

5 Change your computer screensaver and/or wallpaper to a fun message from you; or how about a special photo of you or your family?

6 Here's a tip from a corporate traveler: Rebecca gave her two children Beanie Babies® positioned in prayer. She told them to put the bears on their pillows and they would know that she was saying a prayer for them from wherever she was. It was so comforting for everyone.

7 This idea comes to you from my son, Bryan. "Ever since I've been in kindergarten, Mom had a saying she told me every morning when I left for school. She'd say, 'I love you with my whole life. Have a great day.' Then I turned 16, and she added, 'Drive carefully.' When Mom traveled, I missed hearing it when I walked out the door. She bought a picture frame/clock where you can record a 10-second voice message. She put a picture of the two of us in one side and recorded what she always told me so that I could play it whenever she was on the road. I took it with me to college. Now she can still send me off to classes in the same way she did all through school."

8 Have the kids make a collage that you can take with you. If that's not possible, then you make one about yourself to leave at home. You'll need the following supplies:
- Glue
- Piece of construction paper
- Scissors
- Old magazines or catalogs
- Crayons, pens, or colored pencils

Cut out pictures of things you like and things you like to do, such as fishing, biking, reading, soccer, basketball, and examples of your favorite colors, clothes, movies, cartoon characters, etc. It's your personality. Glue the pictures onto the construction paper in whatever way you want—the crazier the better. Let dry and laminate it or put it in a page protector.

Picture Perfect

When we think of staying in touch, we usually think of using photographs. Digital cameras are great for taking pictures "on the spot" and emailing them right away. Here are great tactics for sharing pictures:

9 You can make your favorite photos into fabric transfers. Put a fabric photo onto tee shirts, hats, or even pillow-cases for your kids. They'd love to "wear" a picture of the two of you.

10 A friend of mine who travels a lot selected six of his favorite photos, scanned them, and printed them onto two sheets of photo paper. He placed them back-to-back in a plastic page protector. It's easier to tuck that page away and have six to eight photos all together.

11 Go to a local copy shop, Office Depot®, or other office supply store that provides a copy service, and create a calendar with a family photo for each month. Then you can use this calendar at home to mark off the days until your serviceman returns.

12 Take a child's school picture and make a refrigerator magnet out of it. The easy way is to buy a magnetic plastic frame and glue little jewels and rhinestones on it or decorate it with paint pens.

Service members can take pictures with them. (One deployed mom slept with her family photos in her pillowcase.) Sometimes the service member can make a video, but needs to get permission through a public release to create one.

13 Here's a contribution from a ninth grade girl: "I keep pictures of my dad while he's away on trips or when I'm just not close to him." This comment makes me think that we, as parents, often carry photos of our children, but how many of our children have been given pictures of *us* to have with them. You can take care of that right now.

14 Cindy Bruschwein, and her 19 month old daughter Sarah, introduce you to *Flat Dave*. Three months after Dave Bruschwein was deployed, Cindy took a "waist up" photo of Dave, dressed in fatigues, to a local print shop. They enlarged it to life size and mounted it on foam board – like a big, two-dimensional paper doll. "He was missing so many family gatherings" said Cindy. Now, *Flat Dave* travels to graduations, weddings, and other celebrations where he takes his rightful place in the photographs. Copies are sent to Dave overseas so he can see where he's traveled. Cindy  keeps an album at home of everywhere *Flat Dave* has been...even tucking Sarah into bed. Speaking of Sarah, the real Dave is about to receive a *Flat Sarah*, minus the foam board, so he can see how much she's grown.

You're My Top Priority

Sometimes it's just enough to do something that says, "You're my top priority." It's a reminder of how important it can be to our families to know that they are always on the top of your mind.

I read that actors Kevin Bacon and Kyra Sedgwick take special care to keep their family close. Whenever possible, Kevin gets up with his kids every morning to take them to school. He's involved in every detail of their lives. With both actors working, it's sometimes a challenge to make time together, so he has instituted a "two week rule" where the family never goes longer than two weeks without all getting together. I also read that Kevin values the time he spends with his kids so much that he won't give out autographs when he's with them because at that moment, they are his top priority.

15 When my son comes home from college for the holidays, there comes a time when he has to return. When Bryan is packing, I go up and sit on his bed just to be there with him. I don't get in the way or try to do anything other than what he specifically asks me to do. I just want to enjoy him one more time before he leaves. You can do the same thing. Spend some time with the person who is leaving by helping him/her pack; but understand that this is an emotional time for everyone, so don't get in the way. It will give you some "alone" time to talk.

16 I heard from a source at a Family Readiness Center that you can show your kids that they are your priority by letting them decorate the inside of your foot locker. Of course, my source also said that eventually it has to be put back to normal. Something else you can do is to think ahead about exactly how else your kids can help you. What could they do to help you get ready? They'll feel so much more a part of everything when they have an actual "job" to do, and they'll know that you really do want them to help.

17 This is especially good when Mom is the "doctor" around the house and she is the one who's gone: Assemble a *Cuts and Scrapes Box* that includes antiseptic, Band-aids® in colors or cartoon characters, a lollypop, and a card with a "Kiss" made with lipstick from you to make it all better.

18 Make copies of basic, simple line drawings from clip art programs, and print them onto one side of white paper. Then put them together to make a coloring book. For additional pages, have a cartoonist make a caricature of each family member (don't forget the family pets) and have these added to the book. You can have a copy center bind it with a comb binding so that it lays flat. Leave the book with your child along with a special box of crayons.

19 Order a subscription to your children's favorite magazine (they have them for all ages) and have it come each month while you're away. They'll think of you every time they read it.

20 Make a personalized rubber stamp that has your child's name on it. He or she can use it to personally stamp every letter written to you.

Here are a couple of ideas about notes:

21 Head out to the store and pick up a bunch of small greeting cards. Both American Greetings® and Hallmark® have at least one series of 99¢ cards—so go crazy. They're small (only about the size of a playing card) so they're perfect for leaving in drawers, purses, shoes, or medicine cabinets just as reminders that "you're my top priority." Hide these cards before you leave so that they're found at different times during your assignment.

22 In addition to the cards, here's something even easier. Before you head out the door, write some special notes on separate small slips of paper. Try writing them on colored construction paper or funny Post-it® notes, too. This is especially great for younger kids because the notes stand out better. Now go around the house and tape these "good morning" notes and sayings on places where they'll be noticed first thing in the morning. Tape them on the inside of the front door, the bathroom mirror, on the car's steering wheel, the coffee maker, and in the refrigerator.

You can prepare some notes and cards ahead of time and leave them with the spouse or caregiver who is remaining home. Have them hide them, or give them out at important times or events that happen in the lives of your family while you're away.

A Conversation with Lisa White

I had the privilege of talking with Lisa White, the youth volunteer for the Colorado Army National Guard's Family Readiness Center. This center is a support agency for deployed soldiers and their families. She is paramount in establishing a youth camp for kids so they can be in an environment with other kids who are experiencing just what they are going through.

As a volunteer, Lisa has gotten together with many husbands and wives to talk about how to stay connected with everyone when one or both parents are deployed. She strives for face-to-face meetings because it allows her to get to know the families she is working with. This lets her learn about their lifestyle so she can customize connection ideas for that family. And customize she does! The most important tip she gives is the importance of *planning ahead.* You can now benefit from some of the wonderful ideas and thoughts that Lisa cared enough to share with us. Enjoy!

23 This idea works well for older boys: Often when Dad is deployed, boys feel like they're the "man of the house" now. The problem is, this often puts too much pressure on them. They feel like they have to take on extra responsibilities, when instead, they need to stay little boys. Lisa's suggestion to help waylay that pressure, but still understand that the feelings of responsibility are important, is to make up a list of what the son can specifically do to be a part of helping the household to run efficiently. This list can include:

- Take out the garbage.
- Get the newspaper every morning.
- Sit next to Mom at the dinner table.
- Answer the front door when someone arrives.

Little kids can take on roles, too, but be sure to make the list together. The big thing is to pre-plan and have open communication. You can set up the same type of list for girls, especially if Mom is deployed.

24 When the wife or husband goes away, there are many emotions that take place at home. This can be confusing for some children, and they're not sure how they should respond. Since kids like lists, make a list of emotions they're bound to feel or observe, and how they might react. Then they'll know what to do. This might look like:

If Mommy feels like this __(sad)___, or does this ___(cry)__, then you can do this __(_____)_ for me, or tell me this __(_____)_.

You can do the same for older kids who often want to deal with their feelings on their own. It's like they're really saying, "Just sit here, hug me, acknowledge me, but leave me alone." This works best for when dads go away because it clears the emotions.

25 "When someone leaves," Lisa says, "it's not just about pictures and notes. It's about everyday life."

The most important thing to remember in the pre-deployment stage is to prepare ahead of time. Be aware of how the normal workings of the household schedule are going to be upset. By thinking of this first, you'll be able to cover for the voids that will be left.

Begin by being aware of the traditions that will change. What if it's a tradition for Dad to take his daughter out for breakfast on her birthday? What happens if he's gone over that birthday? Or if Mom makes it a Friday afternoon tradition to bring home a specific candy bar to her nine-year-old son, and then she ships out? By writing these down and being aware of them, the remaining parent can carry on the tradition. Now Dad at home can bring home the candy bars, or Mom at home can make the birthday breakfast reservations. By recording everything, it makes it a lot easier on the parent left at home. Some other things to write down:

- How the laundry gets done.
- Mom and/or Dad's everyday chores.
- Standard shopping lists for what you buy every week.
- Favorite recipes or dishes. (Ask a neighbor or close friend to have your family's favorite food made and brought over once a week. People like to help.)

26 Strategies that *count down* the time apart help to keep it in perspective. If you know you'll be gone for a long time, write a quick note once a week for your children. Either leave these notes at home with a caregiver to be given out personally, or mail one each Monday—especially if you'll be missing a milestone event.

27 For small children (two to four years old), make a placemat for them. Use drawings, photos of you together, sayings, stickers, or just colored shapes. Make it together and take it to an office supply store or copy center to have it laminated. Then you can be *together* at every meal.

28 Make a picture button pin. You know, the kind that people wear to athletic events, conventions, etc. Most award shops and elementary schools have the equipment available. Get a picture of the soldier in uniform and put a note under the picture that says, "I'm proud of my dad (or mom)." Make the button for the child to wear to school. Most schools would love to be a part of this by helping your child make the button.

29 According to the people I talked with, another great way to stay in touch is by sending *care packages*. Big or small, they're always appreciated. They can arrive anytime and have anything edible in them. Make sure that what you send is wrapped very well to minimize the breakage. Also, realize that shipping times are long so don't send anything that will spoil. Some of the favorite items among soldiers are:

- Any appropriate food
- Beef jerky
- Small packaged snacks
- Candy
- Special traditional homemade goodies
- Grandmas® or Pepperidge Farm® cookies
- Single servings of flavored coffee, teas, or hot chocolate

- The hometown newspaper
- Small pouches of baby wipes (great for low water cleanups, and they smell like home)

Our church sent care packages to all our college freshmen twice during their first year. It was just one more way to let the students know that they have a connection to their home and community. What better way for service personnel to feel connected to their community than to have the church send care packages through the appropriate channels. Can you organize something?

30 When making cookies for care packages, remember to decorate them especially for the parent—it's something the children can do themselves. When you ship the cookies, remember to wrap them well.

Lisa shared a story with me about a family where the kids really wanted to remember their dad's birthday by making him a birthday cake like they did every year. But what good would the cake do at home? Not much—so they mailed it! An iced birthday cake, complete with candles, was boxed and shipped thousands of miles away through the postal system. It certainly paints an interesting picture.

Speaking of pictures, Mom was on top of things enough to take a Polaroid® picture of what the cake looked like *before* it was sent and included it in the box. Why do you think this mom went along with the idea of mailing a cake? "Because," she said, "sometimes you just gotta give in." Good for her!

31 This next idea falls under the "Have a Plan" heading and has to do with schoolwork. Challenges arise when all of a sudden the parent who used to help with this is no longer available. Lisa says the key to keeping schoolwork current is to set up a plan ahead of time. When the spouse who is left at home is not able to help in certain areas (for me it would be math), then find someone who can. Look to grandparents, neighbors, tutors, or their classroom teacher to fill in. Maybe you can even answer some questions during whatever brief phone time you have with them. Lisa says that putting a plan in place ahead of time helps with the fights that arise over homework and even chores around the house.

The following idea fits here, although it's not a part of my conversation with Lisa. It comes under pre-planning. I've discovered that legal and medical issues can become a different kind of problem for families with stepparents. If the parent is deployed and a stepparent is left behind, there could be legal problems for authorizing medical care. An organization of volunteer lawyers developed a *Family Member Pre-deployment Checklist* to help with these and other situations. The website can be found in the back of this book under *Resources and Support*.

32 Consistency in daily lives plays a big role in keeping the peace at home. Sometimes Lisa gets some touchy questions and maybe you've had this happen, too. She talked about an eight-year-old boy who, during his free time, always liked to play Army. When his dad was deployed, his mom thought that maybe it would be better to have him stop playing this game because it was now "too close to home."

However, it was suggested that he should not stop playing because it was a constant in his daily routine—and now it could be a way to stay connected to Dad. Lisa took it a step further and suggested that Dad could be involved by creating some fake "tactical plans" before he leaves—perhaps basing them on football strategies. Then his son could play out these plans with his own army. It's a true connection in the *real* world.

Lisa, thank you for being a part of this project and for giving families in all branches of the military such insightful strategies for staying together—even when separated.

"If you take care of the people,
the people will take care of the mission."
—Sondra Albano, Ph.D.

Chapter 2

Ideas for the Deployment Phase
(during the deployment)

Service families are likely to experience separations stemming from short-notice deployments, frequent active duty assignments and relocations, long hours, shift work and the uncertainty of where they will be next month. While this is an accepted part of a military career, it's not as commonplace for those who are called to duty from civilian forces. Deployment becomes a time of readjustment.

During deployment, many people would say that the most difficult thing to deal with is being separated from their families. It's probably the hardest thing the families have to contend with, too. During this time the miles can seem endless. Learning some of the techniques available for staying connected will help to shorten those miles.

Thinking of You

33 In an interview with Tara, she said that when her husband was overseas she knew he could call once a week for only 15 minutes. What was even more frustrating was that, for security purposes, the call was on an "automatic hang up" timer and would cut off the call at exactly 15 minutes—no matter where they were in the conversation! It was hard to try to think of all she wanted to tell him, such as what bills were paid, what the baby did since the last call, etc.

Here's a good suggestion for dealing with this situation: Buy a tiny spiral notebook and write things down as they occur. Carry the notebook with you. Then when you get the call, you can be efficient with your time.

34 This is my absolute favorite connection idea. You can do it for $1.75 and about 30 seconds of your time. Buy a decal that reflects the branch of service that you're in. It can be either an insignia decal or the spelled out name like a college decal. Then place it in the back window of your car. When you are driving and look in your rearview mirror, it will be a quick, happy reminder of your service member. Believe me, it makes you smile. (I had thought that it would read "backwards" when looking at it in the mirror, but it doesn't.)

35 Shared tastes in music among family members is an emotional way to stay in touch. In certain circumstances, soldiers may be allowed CD players or audiotape players. Most likely, you have one or both at home, too. Burn a couple of CDs or record tapes of special songs from over the years for each of you to play while away. When my son went to college, I made a CD of piano music because Bryan used to fall asleep to that music in the car when he was little. It calms him down and he can play it as background music. Sometimes we'll just burn a few songs and send what we think each other will like.

36 A good tip for a deployed parent is to make up a *Memory Box* filled with special things of yours, as well as things that mean something to your children, so that they can go through it occasionally to feel like you're there. Many of those items will have your "scent" on them, and that's an extremely powerful tool to bring you right into the room.

If you have the time, consider going one step further while creating your *Memory Box*. Spend about an hour with your family and decorate the outside of the box in something fun and colorful. This will make it even more personal. Then, together, collect the special things that will go into the box.

37 Select a pre-set time each day for family members to think about each other for just a moment. This will be your own private "together" time. There is a scene in the animated movie *An American Tail* where the mice characters are separated from each other. At night they look in the sky and know that no matter what, they are together because they are looking at the very same moon.

38 With soldiers and families in different time zones, set one of the clocks in your home to the time zone of where the serviceman is. This makes it easier to look at the clock and think of what they might be doing at that moment.

39 **P.S. I Love You!** It might not be something they admit, but many men report that they enjoy getting affectionate little surprise notes. At the end of those notes add a "P.S." It increases the charm. There's something nostalgic about the P.S. that people respond to. It's that special afterthought like when you were at camp and your mom wrote, *P.S. I love you;* or the note your high school sweetheart slipped into the back of your notebook.

Because I Understand

40 There is one common thread that seems to hold military marriages together through times of separation. One of the best things to do while spouses are overseas is to become part of a support group made up of those who remain at home. Look for people on base. This is a great opportunity to meet with others who truly know what you're going through. Sometimes you feel like the outside world can't possibly understand the magnitude of what you're feeling. You need this group to share the everyday challenges you're experiencing, or when you're feeling out of control. Occasionally you just need a break, and a support group can help by:

- getting together for coffee;
- listening while you just let loose and yell;
- babysitting so you can get away on your own;
- sharing what they know about services available;
- exchanging good fiction books;
- sending encouragement via email by forwarding inspirational messages to each other; or
- hosting social events to cement your connection as a continuous support network.

Remember that support systems are only effective if they are used. Most military spouses who remain behind are gifted with a tremendous amount of spirit and courage. They feel a sense of acceptance that "this is what we do." But even with that self-sufficiency, please take advantage of these support groups. They'll be enormously helpful during the times when you find that your "acceptance attitude" is waning; and when you're feeling positive, that spirit will be a lifting force for others.

41 A third grade class at a local elementary school wrote letters to Tara's husband in the service and sent him oatmeal cookies in a care package! He loved it. Are you a teacher and can your class do the same thing for a service man or woman?

42 Buy your child's favorite cookies or small pieces of candy like a Hershey's Kiss® or peanut M&M's®. When they miss you, tell them they are allowed to eat **just one** candy or cookie. (Limits are advisable.)

43 When my son was young, he always had a "Hug Friend" around. This was a special stuffed animal just for the purpose of hugging whenever I wasn't there and he felt he needed to hug something. Since our sense of smell is an effective connector, you might "spritz" the stuffed animal with some of your perfume or after shave.

44 Family Support Services Centers usually offer suggestions for stress management. When you're the one left behind, you have to realize how imperative it is for you to learn how to do little things for yourself that help to lessen your own stress. Is there a Health and Wellness Center (HAWC) near you, maybe on base? The concept is fairly new and they're popping up all over. These centers provide information and services that will keep you fit and mentally/emotionally together during the separation.

One woman related that she thinks these centers are the military's best kept secret, and for now she's glad because then there's never a wait at the massage chair! She packs her three little ones in the car and heads over there about once a week. The babysitting service watches the kids while she gets a 45-minute stress relieving massage in a warm and relaxing atmosphere. This is HER time and she deserves it. She says that more spouses should give this a try.

Spouses...Are You Listening?

Many of the ideas in this book involve how to stay connected to the children. That's important because it's difficult for younger children to actually understand the logic behind the deployment. They just know that their moms or dads are gone. With spouses, it's another matter. There's a special kind of love that's missing for a while. The void that's left is on another level.

In interviews with Tara and Julie-ann, I learned that they're married to wonderful men who took the time to find unique ways to show how much they care when they're on assignment. I'm pleased to have permission to share these ideas with you. As a spouse who is either leaving or staying behind, you can personalize the following suggestions to the particular needs of your own relationship.

45 Julie-ann loves the little Reese's Peanut Butter Cups®. Sometimes it just takes one to satisfy her craving for a taste of chocolate. Dave knows this. When he's on an assignment that takes him away for one or two weeks, he buys one peanut butter cup for each day he's away. Before he leaves, he hides them around the house so he knows Julie-ann won't find them. Then, each night when he's able to quickly phone home, he tells her where **just one** peanut butter cup is hidden. He said that if he told her all the hiding places at once, she'd eat them all! What a great way to make each call special.

46 Write a *Legacy Letter*. This is where you start a few sentences of a letter when you get up in the morning and then add sentences throughout the day when you have something special to say. This legacy letter can be composed over a week's time to give you more time to work on it. At the end of the day—or week—you've written a legacy that makes your spouse feel like they've been with you all day long.

47 When service members are on TDY they sometimes are given a per diem amount of money to help with food and extra expenses. On occasion, David found himself with a little bit left over at the end of a day. He popped this change in an envelope. Then when he returned home, he gave his wife the spare change he collected as a gift and encouraged her to go buy something little and frivolous with it.

48 A friend of mine did this for her college student, but it will work just as well in your situation. She got it out of a magazine and called it a *Heart Attack*. She cut lots of different sizes of hearts out of colored construction paper. Then she wrote a *love phrase* (such as "You Doll" or "Cutie" or "Love Me") on each heart just like the little candy valentine hearts. She put about 50 or so in a big envelope and mailed it. When her husband pulled out all these hearts, it was like big *love* confetti.

49 Dave set up a *treasure hunt* around the house before he shipped out. He bought his wife a special gift that he hid in the house. Then he designed a series of clues, each one leading to another, until she eventually found the gift. On one of his phone calls home, he helped her guess the location of the first clue. She found it before he hung up, then had fun completing the treasure hunt after the phone call—prolonging the connection.

50 Here's one for the spouse who remains at home. Record an audiotape reflecting on all your favorite romantic memories—*the time we danced in bare feet on the roof of our apartment building; the moment Jimmy was born and I touched your cheek; etc.* It's just between the two of you, so anything goes.

51 Start a *Grateful Journal*. It's simple. Set up a computer file, or use a nice blank journal from the bookstore. Each day write three different things that you appreciate about your spouse. At the end of the week, email or *snail mail* that list to them.

52 This idea is a variation of the *Grateful Journal*. "Once when David was on TDY for six weeks," shares Julie-ann, "he kept a daily journal of his happenings and thoughts about me. Then he gave it to me when the six weeks were over. It was a very special gift!"

53 When one airman was on a shorter assignment that took him away for five nights, he prearranged to have five different people (one for each day) help him with his plan. Sometime during each day he was gone, he had a different person call or stop by their home to say that he loved her and missed her. At first it was a complete surprise, but his wife finally caught on to his scheme after a couple of days and looked forward to hearing from her husband through his next messenger.

Let's Get Personal

It's difficult when you can't be there in person to experience the day-to-day changes that occur at home. Here are some ideas for audio and video recording, as well as journaling, to help your soldier be a part of all that happens:

54 Do you have a new baby? Have the spouse at home make an audio (or digital) recording of your baby's laughter while he or she is doing something fun. It's such a warm and wonderful sound. Along with the recording, include a written description of what activity the baby is doing that's sparking all of that delightful laughter.

55 The hardest thing about being away is missing milestones in a child's life. If your spouse is gone for your child's first haircut, tie a ribbon around a lock of hair and send it with a picture of the child getting the haircut.

56 If there's a baby or toddler at home, be sure to leave a video camera so your child's milestones can be recorded. Also, record what's happened in your child's growth while you were separated. That will make a great home movie for *Movie Night* when your soldier returns!

57 This idea is from Rebecca, who travels about half of her time for business. Although she may not be gone for extended periods of time the way a soldier would, she's away much more often. "We started a journal for the kids to write in every day to let us know what they are doing. They write their thoughts on something they're happy or sad about, something that happened at school or home, etc. When I get home, it's a way to catch up on what happened while I was gone."

58 Along with Rebecca's idea, kids also might keep a journal of their accomplishments, awards, grades, etc. Have them write down some things that they want to do with the parent when he or she gets home. Writing things down tends to insure that they're not forgotten.

59 Try *Two-part Journaling*. It's very helpful to keep a journal of what you do together as it refers to a child's progress growing up. Because you're not together on a day-to-day basis, this serves as a reminder of the small steps that happen between the members of the family. It acts as cement for the times when you're not living together. The first part of the journaling is done while the soldier/parent is deployed. The second part is done when he/she returns by continuing to write in it together whenever possible.

It's a Communication Thing

Technology makes sending emails one of the best ways to stay connected. These pages talk about emails and telephones. It's a quick way to connect, and from my interviews, the most effective. Some phone calls are short, some are timed, and some are longer. But no matter what the length, nothing beats hearing the voice of the person you love.

Email is an incredible *real time* method of staying connected in a way that we haven't had available in past times of conflict. You can instantly send home words, images, and the security that your hands, or the hands of your loved one, were on the keyboard only moments earlier, which means that you're alive and well. However, it can also pose some security challenges through inadvertent leaks of secure information. In the months ahead, branches of the military may begin to limit, monitor, or block some communications that could appear sensitive; however, for the time being, email is a marvelous source for providing instantaneous connections from the field to relatives back home. It's a wonderful morale booster, so consider it one of your best forms of contact.

60 My challenge to you is to see if you can make those emails different. Break out of the mold within the realms of security restrictions. Send something funny, maybe a little outrageous, or something that the recipient would never expect. You might consider setting up a special phrase or saying that's just for your family, and include it in every email. You don't need to do something outrageous every time, just when you want a special pick-me-up.

61 If you're on assignment in the States, get instant messaging on your computers. Then you can set times to chat in *real time* over the computer. I love being online in the middle of the day, hearing the chimes, and finding a message from my son. It's as good as a phone call, but you have to know when and where it's appropriate.

62 For emails, create an age-appropriate, fun quiz or questionnaire for your child to do when he/she signs on. Here are some suggestions for what might be included:

- Current events
- Friends
- Interests
- Activities
- Other favorite things

Make the quiz easy, so they can't fail. People love to do quizzes. That's why short online quizzes and surveys are so popular. Remember back in school when you used to pass notes that had quiz questions that your best friend answered about your current crush?

63 Many Family Service Centers are exploring the idea of buying video cams to hook up to computers to allow for the taping of brief, personal video greetings that can be emailed overseas. Contact your unit's Service Center or Readiness Center to see if it's available for you.

64 For emails, have each of you answer the question: "What would you do with a million dollars?" Email your answers to each other. You might add something like, "You must have at least one truly goofy idea."

65 Children can formulate questions for their deployed parent to help de-mystify the destination and the daily experience. For example, "How many sandbags a day can you fill?" or "How hot does it get at night where you are?"

Tip: A great resource for questions is *The Kid's Book of Questions* by Gregory Stock. Parents may want to get to know their kids better (and vice versa) by asking some of these questions before or during the deployment, either by phone or email. Some examples of questions:

- When someone says you are just like your mom or dad, do you like it?
- Do you try to be more like your parents or different from them?
- What was the most exciting thing you ever did on a dare? Are you glad you did it?

66 Along with emails, remember that you can also email greeting cards. There are lots to choose from and often include fun animation and sounds. One of my favorite sites for online cards is www.bluemountainarts.com. There's a tab for email cards on the home page. Try one—it's addictive.

67 If your cell phone doesn't have long distance included, or if extreme distances forbid it, send prepaid long distance cards. Some are designed to be used from anywhere in order to make your connection easier and more frequent. You may find these cards most applicable to stateside assignments. At the time of writing this, the best deals I found were Sam's Club (from 2¢ to 5¢ per minute) and at Diamond Shamrock gas stations where you can buy 1,000 minutes for about $20. Military calling cards are also available for phone calls overseas. Check with your Family Center to locate a sponsoring organization.

Zits and all associated characters: ©2002 Zits Partnership.

68 What else can you do on the phone? Talk to the kids before you leave and make a favorite song *your* song. When you call home, get the kids on the phone and sing your song together. One family chose *You Are My Sunshine*. It's simple, short, and filled with joy. That may stick in their minds, and yours—even more than words. You just may be an inspiration to those standing in line behind you waiting to use the phone!

69 From computer programmer Carl Carlson, "If the cell phones your family use have text messaging, you can just leave a quick text message that says *I Love You,* and it doesn't require a response." Again, you can only do this where appropriate.

Finally, I offer some words of advice for using those precious 20 minutes of phone time. Each of you is having a difficult time with the separation. The spouse at home is dealing with the kids, illnesses, news, household questions, and loneliness. The deployed spouse is dealing with care and concern, fear of the unknown, and loneliness. Please be aware that it's hard to solve huge problems in this short time frame and could possibly leave you both uneasy. Hearing an uplifting voice on the other end of the phone, however, can do wonders for helping a soldier get through the rest of the day. These are 20 important minutes, so know ahead of time what you plan to talk about and be aware of the effect your words will have—both positive and negative. My advice is "Be aware and take care."

Fun Projects for
Getting the Kids Involved

You are the bows from which your
children as living arrows are sent forth.
The archer sees the mark
upon the path of the infinite,
and He bends you with his might that His
arrows may go swift and far.

Let your bending in the
Archer's hand be for gladness:
For even as He loves the arrow that flies,
so He loves also the bow that is stable.

—Kahlil Gibran from *The Prophet*

This is one of my favorite sections. I know that it's difficult to be away from your spouse when you leave because you miss the closeness that comes from being lovers. But you always know that your spouse, in a logical sense, understands the need for you to be away. With children, it's a different story. They may not understand. They just know that you're gone. What makes it even harder is the fact that young children don't have a very good sense of the reality of time. You can be gone for one week or one year and it's all the same to them.

The following is a wonderful way to help bridge the concept of time for the young ones:

70 Get a large empty jar (about the size of a quart of mayonnaise) and wash and dry it thoroughly. Here's what you put in the jar: For every day that the sailor will be gone, place one marble in the jar. If he/she will be deployed for a year, then you'll place 365 colorful marbles in the jar. Then, beginning the day after the sailor leaves, have the child take one marble from the jar every day. As the level of marbles goes down, the closer it is to the time your loved one will be home. Here are some variations to what you might put in the jar:

- Pieces of wrapped hard candies
- Peanut M&M's®
- Hershey's Kisses®
- Colored gum balls

For children under age three, make a paper chain where one link represents each day of the assignment. To count down the time, tear off a link each day.

Now let's look at a few things you might not have thought of—and even how the phone can make your child feel special. These are projects that kids can do so they will feel that their deployed parent will truly have a piece of them while away.

71 Another idea from Lisa White: Keep sending photographs, emails, and letters home. "Kids like pictures taken of the words *I love you*." How can you do that? Write it in shaving cream on a mirror, or draw it on paper or in the sand, and then take a picture of it. Maybe you can even spell it out in chocolate, pebbles, or pennies. Kids can be involved by using sidewalk chalk to write it on the driveway. Take a picture and send it to Dad or Mom.

72 If your child is just learning to write, have him or her write "I Love You" with a crayon on paper in their own distinctive handwriting. The recipient will love it!

73 Give your school-age child a disposable camera and have him/her take pictures of weekday or weekend activities. The more fun the better. Others can help by taking pictures of him/her in class, playing a sport, etc. Have the photos developed and send them in the order in which they were taken—to be a part of "A day in the life of...."

74 This is nice for pre-teens or teens: Write a short letter to your child relaying some of your thoughts about the time they were born and the events of the day leading up to it, such as who was doing what, etc. Bryan has always loved to hear about how his dad was playing baseball when I had to go to the hospital, how he was born one minute before midnight, and how he was *almost* an Easter baby. This story never grows old.

75 Take young children out on a *treasure hunt* around the yard. Tell them to look for things that their soldier mom or dad might enjoy. This probably will include simple things like colorful leaves, small stones, blades of grass, etc. Put these together and send them. Don't discredit anything that a child finds, with the possible exception of something alive—like a caterpillar!

To:

Elaine Dumler
6460 W. 98th Court
Westminster, CO 80021

Thank you...
for your service and
commitment, whether
on assignment or here at
home as a family member.

Name

Address

City, State, Zip

Tell us...

How does **YOUR** family stay connected? Would you share your special idea with us? We'd like to know for future editions of the book, or to tell others in a monthly "tips and ideas" email newsletter.

♥ Write your idea, then stamp and mail the postcard.

_____

_____

_____

_____

_____

_____

Check here: ☐ yes, please share my idea!   ☐ Yes, you can use my name
☐Yes, please email me the free monthly "tips and ideas" newsletter.

My email is: _____

76 I remember when Bryan was in grade school, he would always come home with a joke he had heard that day on the tip of his tongue. Remember those? They were the simple little jokes that kids thought were the funniest thing they had heard all day. Have your child write them down and email a "joke of the day" to the service member.

77 Have a favorite family sticker (like a fun sun, cartoon character, flower, bird, etc.) and make sure everyone has some. Then put one on every letter you send to each other. You might even stick one on the outside of the envelope. You can find some really cool ones at stores that sell scrapbooking materials or from a company called Creative Memories®. (To locate a Creative Memories® consultant, you may visit www.creativememories.com.) And don't forget to seal your letter with a big kiss! Use lipstick or tinted gloss to make it even better.

78 For pre-teens or older children: Write down a short list of "Best advice I got from...(Mom or Dad)" and email or *snail mail* the list to the parent. This kind of thing makes them feel super good. It lets them know that even from a distance, they are able to have influence on what their children learn.

More Fun Stuff and Projects

One of the best ways for children to keep the connection with deployed parents (and to know that their parents are thinking of them, as well) is to make them something that they can take with them. This section will show you projects for kids, fun ways to use *snail mail,* and tips for helping your child to get involved.

79 In our busy lives, it can sometimes be seen as a burden on our time to gather all the necessary materials for our children when they come to us saying, "I want to make something." It's easier to say, "Not now," than to hunt for the paper, paints, scissors, crayons, etc. So be ready ahead of time for all of the projects that your child may want to do on the spur of the moment. Assemble a *Craft Box* with everything they will need to be creative. Then when they get the call to create, they can get out the box, spread out a plastic tablecloth, and be ready to dig in. A large shoebox will serve as a *treasure chest* for everything they need. Here are some things you might want to include:

- Construction paper
- White copier paper
- School glue
- Scissors
- Pieces of felt
- Scraps of fabric and lace
- Buttons
- Sequins

- Glitter
- Pipe cleaners
- Macaroni shapes
- Paintbrushes
- Watercolor paint set
- Tissue paper
- Ribbons
- Wiggle eyes
- Rhinestones
- Small yarn pompoms
- Pieces of yarn
- Paper doilies
- Variety of stickers (hearts, stars, etc.)

You'll be amazed at the wonderful cards and projects that will come out of all this creativity. Projects are a wonderful way to make time go by—especially when you're missing someone.

80 Help your kids create their own stationery to use for special notes. Make it a simple self-mailer with lines for writing and a clip art picture from a computer publisher program. Print it on card stock paper, and you're all set to write. Personal stationery also makes a great gift to give to your child.

81 Have your teenagers use their computer skills to create a family newsletter, either online or on paper. Make it one page and fill it with events from the family. Include an interview with a grandparent, movie reviews, question of the week, list of birthdays, jokes, or just thoughts of the day. Put an issue out every couple of weeks or every month.

82 Write your dad or mom a limerick especially for him her and put it in his/her duffel bag, foot locker, or pocket. You can also mail it. A limerick is a short poem. It's easy to write because it only has five lines. Limericks are *supposed* to be funny, so you really can't go wrong.

Here's how they are formatted: the 1st, 2nd and 5th lines rhyme with each other, and the 3rd and 4th lines rhyme with each other. It's easy to start because they usually begin with: "There once was a...." Here are a couple of examples:

I once had a son at K.U.,
who thought that his meals were too few.
So he packed a big lunch,
and he started to munch,
and missed three classes before he was through!

—OR—

I once had a dad who was a magician—
when he could have been a physician.
But when we were down,
he could make laughter from frowns,
and we were healthier from this transition!

See? It isn't that difficult to do. Help the kids out with the first couple, then let them head into the project on their own. Just remember that nothing is wrong—and the funnier the better.

Email might be the fastest way to get a message home, but it isn't necessarily the most fun. For that, you have to be creative with *snail mail*. Years ago, that's all we baby boomers had available to us when we got mail.

When I was about 10 to 12 years old, I spent two weeks every summer at camp. My dad wrote me letters that I would get almost every day. That was how we stayed connected. What I liked best about his letters was that they were far from the ordinary. He did some interesting things with a pencil and paper. In fact, his letters were so much fun that other kids in my tent wanted to read them, too! When you're away long enough to send *snail mail*, try at least one of these approaches. Your kids will love it, and it will keep them busy for quite a while.

83 **Puzzle letters:** The simplest way to write this type of letter is to get out a sheet of plain copy paper, sit down, and write your letter. When you're finished, take a pair of scissors and cut it into about 15 odd shapes. If you don't have scissors readily available, you can tear it into pieces. Then put these pieces into an envelope and mail it home. Your child will have to put the *puzzle* together in order to read your letter.

Here's another alternative that the children can use for sending letters to you. I found a company called *Compoz-A-Puzzle* that manufactures a lightweight white cardboard pre-assembled jigsaw puzzle with about 9-24 pieces. Write a letter on this blank puzzle and then break the pieces apart and mail them. This paper comes in different sizes and with different sized pieces. You may contact them at:

- Compoz-A-Puzzle, Inc.
  Glen Head, NY 11545
  1-800-343-5887
  www.compozapuzzle.com

Here are two products carried by this company that can be used in variations of the above:

Puzzle Clonzz: Pre-assembled jigsaw puzzles that can be used with your computer's laser or inkjet printer.

Adrawables: These are great for kids who want to make something fun to send to you. They are "color-in" jigsaw puzzle greeting cards. The card fronts get colored in and signed, then broken apart and mailed. They come in different card collections like greetings, dinosaurs, spacecraft, sweet-hearts, and Christmas. These are perfect for children who like coloring books.

Another tip from the Family Readiness Center: When you write letters to a service member, number the letters *and* the envelopes in the order they were written. Sometimes the mail causes lots of letters to arrive at once, and the numbering system will alert the recipient to the order in which they were written. They'll make more sense!

84 Using Puzzle Clonzz, make a *real* jigsaw puzzle. Print a photo on a puzzle page, break it apart, and put it in a small box or envelope. Send it to your soldier or include it in a care package.

85 If you have a child over the age of about seven or eight, write and send a note to him/her in an easy, cryptic code (sort of like a cryptogram) with each letter being represented by the respective number of that letter in the alphabet.

A	B	C	D	E	F	G	H	I	J	K	L	M
1	2	3	4	5	6	7	8	9	10	11	12	13

N	O	P	Q	R	S	T	U	V	W	X	Y	Z
14	15	16	17	18	19	20	21	22	23	24	25	26

Here's an example:

8 9   11 1 18 12 1,
   9   13 9 19 19   25 15 21,   1 14 4
12 15 22 5   25 15 21!
   12 15 22 5,   13 15 13 13 25

It says:

Hi Karla,
   I miss you, and love you!
      Love, Mommy

86 Another thing my dad did for me was to take a piece of copy paper and fold the edges and sides around to form an odd shape. Then he'd write his letter to me on this folded paper. When done, he opened the paper and sent it opened up or folded just once or twice. In order for me to read it, I'd have to figure out how to refold the letter the same way that he did. It made receiving mail a real adventure.

Remember that these connection ideas are great for any caregiver to use. If both parents are deployed, then you might be using them from a grandparent's point of view, or a caring neighbor, aunt or uncle, or brother or sister. The important thing is that you're spending time together to be a part of someone else's life.

The only thing we've found that makes the emptiness bearable is each other.

—from the movie Contact

Chapter 3

Post-deployment...and Beyond
(getting back on track)

Getting back on track might not be as easy as it sounds. The best part is that you are all together again, and now it's time to get on with your family life. Things happened while you were gone, as they had to in order for your home to continue to run itself. Responsibilities changed and sometimes people had to change, too, in order to meet the needs of the household.

The spouse who remained home discovered that he/she really could balance the checkbook, call in repairmen, do the cooking, get all the kids to where they had to go and when, and make the available money last for the expected length of time. Those successes make people feel good about who they are and what they can accomplish when the need arises; however, feelings of inadequacy may develop if it didn't go as well as planned.

You're home now, so everything can return to *normal*—whatever that is—but probably not right away. There

53

will be a transition period where you'll become "reacquainted" again as a family. Take time to observe your children in their everyday routines, and slowly allow yourself to become a part of those routines again.

You'll need to reacquaint yourself again with your spouse, too. Talk about how everything got done at home in your absence. See what worked and what didn't. Maybe things don't have to go right back to the way they were; it might not be the best solution. The key is to share your expectations with each other. Do you want to hand over the checkbook right away, or did you find that you enjoyed that responsibility and would like to continue to be an active part of your family's financial planning? Is it more difficult than you expected to hand back control of the house when you did such a good job with it yourself? Don't keep all your thoughts secret, but do allow for some "welcome home" time to pass as you bask in the rediscovery of each other. We'll start with a few ideas designed to help you begin the reconnection process.

87 How about starting with 1001 ideas! Get a copy of *1001 Ways to be Romantic* by Gregory Godek. You'll find it at most bookstores or on Amazon.com. From simple ideas like writing "I love you" on the bathroom mirror with a piece of soap, to filling your lover's car with balloons, to more *steamy* ideas when you're ready— it will help turn your marriage back into a love affair!

88 Create a book of coupons for redemption upon your return. Some suggestions: For kids—movie with Mom or Dad, candy bar of your choice, Dairy Queen® trip, making their favorite dinner, or out to their favorite restaurant. For spouse—time together, hugs and kisses (or more), favorite romantic dinner, doing one of the spouse's chores around the house, etc.

89 Did you know that you can name a star after someone? That sounds like the ultimate tribute. If you want to know more, contact the National Star Registry at 1-800-282-3333. Or you can do everything online at www.nationalstarregistry.com.

90 Start now to create a book of entries entitled "The most important thing I learned today." Compile these lessons and give the *book of knowledge* to your child upon graduation from high school. It will always go with him/her as a foundation for whatever avenue he/she chooses to take.

91 Notes are great for the kids, too. Write notes of encouragement for a project or activity they're tackling in school. Put them in their lunch boxes or on their pillows at night. Start with shorter notes for younger children, and then you can get more involved as they grow older. Another option is to write these notes ahead of time and give them to your spouse or even a nanny or sitter to place them around the house to be found when they get home from school.

Home Remedies:
Traditions to Build at Home

**67% of Americans say "I love you" to
someone every day.**

Establishing family traditions is like building the
foundation for your house. It supports everything else
that happens. In order to be gone with less guilt, you
have to feel good about the strength of the family
situation that you're leaving. (I know that I feel
uncomfortable and awkward about heading out for a
speaking engagement if I've just had an argument with
my husband or I'm in discord with my son.) We have
activities that we do on a regular basis while everyone
is home. They're things that can be relied upon—the
foundation.

Do you sometimes feel like your life is overfilled when
you're home? Does it feel like you're living in a *virtual
family*? Do conversations with your kids depend on how
well you've memorized their email addresses and cell
phone numbers? Family togetherness need not be an
impossibility. Traditions are the insights that make
togetherness commonplace.

92 Set aside a night every two weeks as a *Family
Movie Night* or a *Family Game Night*, depending
on the ages of your children. *Movie Night* means that
you rent a family-appropriate movie, make a big bowl of
popcorn and maybe some creamy hot chocolate, and then

snuggle into an evening of movie watching together. It's even better if you can force yourself to not answer the phone during the movie!

Family Game Night involves the same popcorn and hot chocolate, but now you get out a board game or card game that the family can play together. Games are designed for all ages, so no one needs to feel left out. *Game Night* is best for children four years and older. The two favorite games in our household for young children were Candyland®, full of colors and shapes, and Pizza Party®, where each player tries to fill their cardboard slice of pizza with all the cardboard goodies! Then we grew into Sorry!® Life®, and Scrabble®.

93 Make a *Family Video Night*, but not to watch rented video movies. Instead, get out your family home videos and watch those! It's sure to bring some laughter into the room, and it's something that everyone will want to watch.

94 A 13-year old boy gave this suggestion: "For a family to stay together, I think they need to have a family talk. It could take place anywhere and for however long you want it to be. Family talks help you solve problems inside and outside of the house."

95 Have a special "date" between each parent and each child. This is his or her own personal time alone with that parent. Maybe go to dinner and a movie, or a museum, the zoo, shopping, children's concert, or other individual interest. The "dates" that my dad and I had were when I spent hours working with just him while he edited our 8mm home movies. I was the one who narrated them on the sound stripping, and I helped him create titles for the segments. He went all out with our movies—and I was a big part of it; but best of all was that it was *our time* together. One of my friends had *Date Night* with her dad, too. Their favorite activity was going to play miniature golf and then off to Dairy Queen® for an ice cream cone dipped in chocolate!

96 *Date Night* with Dad (or Mom) is great, but what about *Date Night* with your spouse? Whenever her husband was home, Julie-ann said they had a special night set aside for *Date Night* once a week. And even though it didn't always work out that often, that's what they tried for. Here's what she said about it: "Fight for it! Even if it's just out for an extended cup of coffee. Plan ahead or it will never happen. Have the babysitter all lined up even if you don't know where the two of you are going. It's important to budget for your *Date Nights*, too. If you don't set aside the money for at least the sitter, then it's too easy to find excuses."

There are advantages to a *Date Night*:

- It gives you an important time to reconnect and refuel for the next trip away from home.

- Making it a priority helps to relieve some of the guilt that exists with having to leave.
- An added benefit is that the whole family sees your commitment to each other, and that adds a secure feeling to the household.

Let's talk about Birthdays!

97 Birthdays were always special in my home as I was growing up. That entire day was *ours,* and everyone in the family helped to make it that way. Try one of our birthday traditions: We asked each family member to name his or her favorite dinner and cake—and it sometimes changed a bit every few years. Then on each of our birthdays, we were able to pick the entire menu, along with our favorite cake. My favorite meal was steak, cheese potatoes, and green beans—topped off with a spice cake with caramel frosting!

98 Here's another tradition that involves birthdays and creating a healthier family. Being lured into cigarette smoking is a challenge that teenagers of all generations seem to face. My dad found a creative way to deter us from smoking until we were at least old enough to make an intelligent decision for ourselves, instead of being influenced by peers. It involves another common thread that transcends generations—the importance of money to a teenager.

We were encouraged not to try smoking during the year. Then on each birthday from ages 13 to 18, after dinner Dad would ask the birthday boy or girl the following question, "Have you smoked a cigarette in the past year?" We would answer yes or no—usually no. When we said no, we were given $20—$1 for each cigarette in a pack. There was enough trust in our family that the question was always answered truthfully. I know this because on my sister's 16th birthday, she answered "yes" knowing that she was forfeiting the money.

Here's the creative part—he never gave us just a $20 bill, but individual new, crisp $1 bills packaged in fun ways. On my 17th birthday I opened a box to find a pack (flip-top) of cigarettes where all the tobacco had been carefully emptied from each one. Then a $1 bill was rolled exceptionally small and placed in each of the cigarette papers in place of the tobacco! That was cool.

99 From an eighth grader: "When my brother and I have our birthdays, we make homemade ice cream and celebrate."

100 Wouldn't it be nice to know exactly what your kids enjoy about your time together? Especially in families where children's lives are overscheduled, ask the kids to sit and answer the question: "If your mom and dad could give you three things, what would they be?" Most of the time the *things* suggested will actually be variations of activities. If you don't get that response (if the kids are too little) try asking the question: "If you could do any three things you want with Mom and Dad, what would they be?" Usually the answers will involve how your children prefer to spend time with you, and then you can focus your activities to meet the specific needs of your kids.

In My Opinion...
Top 10 List of
What Worked in My Family

1. The stronger your relationships are at home, the easier it is when you have to be away.

2. **Talk** to your kids about everything and anything.

3. **Listen** to your kids about everything and anything.

4. **Please, know who their friends are.** Even beyond this, create bonds with the parents of their friends so that all of you are watching for changes in your child's behavior or attitudes. This can be the first sign of problems, and it's often easier for someone outside of the family to observe first.

5. Care enough to discipline—properly and appropriately.

6. Remember that they miss you as much as you miss them.

7. Respect your kid's tastes—in music, clothes, hairstyles, etc. But remember: **You still know best.** Be willing to establish guidelines together.

8. Pick your battles!

9. Let your children make choices, but help them to understand the concept of consequences. They can take responsibility, too.

10. Say, "I'm proud of you!" often.

There's nothing quite like your family
needing you, and you being able to
come through for them.

Chapter 4

Out of the Mouths of Babes...
What the Kids Said

I talked with a lot of people while preparing the material for this book, and many wonderful ideas were shared by caring people who wanted to make a difference in families. I expected and received ideas from parents and other adults; but I also went directly to the children to hear what they thought. A lot of what was shared has transcended generations, being passed along from grandparents to parents to children. So it's no surprise that a lot of these ideas latch on to tradition. What did surprise me, though, were the number of times that children themselves expressed a strong need for traditions.

As parents, we often think that our kids want to spend as little time as possible with their "out of touch" parents before heading out the door to play the starring role in the rest of their lives. I discovered that this is not so. Most children actually like being with their folks. I liked my parents because they were different. When I was about 12, some of those differences proved to be a bit embarrassing, but as I became a young adult and eventually a parent myself, I valued those differences as a foundation for a stable family.

By day my parents were college professors. By night, Dad was a magician and my mother was Wilbur—his loyal but klutzy rabbit. (And I came from a functional family!) They did magic shows for children and presented these shows at many elementary schools. Growing up in the days of live television, I recall that one of our traditions involved being on television on Christmas morning. I thought that *everyone* spent Christmas morning in a television studio, but I guess not. My parents were on the morning schedule of *Romper Room*, a children's variety show, to do their magic act. All four of us kids were in the studio audience watching. We'd get home shortly after noon and that's when our Christmas morning would really begin. It was fun to be a part of that magic—at least until I was in sixth grade.

That year the magic show was brought to *my* school, and what was once "cool" was now invading my territory. I sat in the auditorium slumping down into my folding chair in utter embarrassment as I watched this magician try to conjure up his bumbling rabbit from a giant black hat. I didn't want anyone to know that those were my parents up there—at least, not until the boy sitting next to me turned in excitement and said, "Wow! Aren't they great?" Great? *My* parents? It was then that I realized he was right. They *were* great, and they were *my* parents—for better or worse! From that time on I was willing to be proud of my parents, and proud that other people liked them, too. Our home was always open to groups of kids, and we shared lots of our own traditions with other families. Now that's a legacy.

So let's hear from those who are the next generation's purveyors of the legacy. Take to heart what they have to share and observe what's important to *them*.

101 A 15-year-old boy shares, "A lot of times our family sits down and watches a movie together. Sometimes we go out to eat and talk about what's going on in our lives. Once a week we also have a family meeting and we have a short discussion from the Bible, then talk about stuff. That's about it, but it's effective."

102 Thoughts from a 16-year-old: "The prolonged absence of a parent really emphasizes the importance of the time that is shared. In that sense, it seems that a tight-knit family permanently instills good values. Family dinners and occasional vacations together are things that have really helped to keep my family tight."

103

An 11-year-old boy says, "Whenever I call my parents—no matter how much work they have, they always talk to me."

104

This started me thinking about the numerous times our kids have a question, ask us for a favor, or need something, but we're too busy to give it much time. The first answer out of our mouths seems to be, "No." And why is that? Usually because we don't have the time or don't want to be bothered by their request. Eventually they just get tired of asking, or they may even start to argue—endlessly. I hate those fights. Whenever members of my family were fighting, it upset everything else that was going on in the house.

I discovered a tactic when Bryan was about 12 that I wish I had learned earlier because it would have saved me a lot of grief. I decided that when he asked me something that required permission, I would make my first answer *Yes* unless there was a real reason to say *No*, such as being unsafe, unreasonable, or too expensive.

Please understand that I didn't become a permissive parent, just one who actually gave thought to my child's requests. Here's the difference:

Before, if Bryan would ask to go to a friend's house, and my answer was *No*, it was usually because of some inconvenience to me. Maybe I just didn't want to drive him there at that moment, so I'd get an argument from him. What changed? With this new thought process, whenever Bryan asked to go to a friend's, I'd think it through to see if there was any reason that he couldn't go, such as it being too close to dinner or something. I began saying *Yes* in those circumstances where I discovered that there was no reason to say *No*.

He began to realize that I'd grant permission when I could, and when I did say *No,* I had real reasons. A wonderful benefit to this was that the arguing stopped because he knew I cared enough to listen and consider what he wanted. Is this something you might try? If it lessens the arguments at home, it's worth the price of this book!

I'm taking a break here to share a poem with you. It made me think about how much we parents tend to get wrapped up in our own day-to-day lives and don't pay as much attention as we should to the activities of our kids. Most kids notice that.

The following poem was written by Molly Waneka, who was a high school senior at the time. She wrote it in the week following the student shootings at Columbine High School in Colorado. Every parent should read it.

Innocence

Did you notice what I was wearing to school today?
Did you even bother to look my way?
Did you realize it might be your last chance
to give your child one...last...glance?

As soon as I step out that door
I am exposed to the world's deadly roar.
You have taught me not to be frightened,
but what about the other kids' parents, who aren't
    quite as enlightened?

Do I have the chance of being in danger
and in the path of someone's release of anger?
Is there anything else you expect of me?
Because I expect the world to have more sanity.

At the end of the day, will we all return home?
Or because of the insanity, will someone be left alone?
When I go outside, is it okay to laugh?
Or will I be breaking the silence of some tragedy's
aftermath?

Can a child still have dreams and goals
without first being frightened for the safety of their
    souls?
Can I have your word that I can live another day?
Or is that a subject in which you have no say?

Did you notice what I was wearing to school today?
Did you even bother to look my way?
Did you realize it might be your last chance
to give your child one...last...glance?

Thanks, Molly, for reminding us always that life is fragile and we all have to remember to take the time to pay attention to each other—parents and children alike. And most people do, as the following will show:

105 An eighth grade boy admits, "When I have an overnight at my friend's house and I miss my mom, I call her to see if she's doing okay." (And you thought that only parents missed their kids!)

106 A ninth grade boy adds, "When my mom or dad goes on a trip, and I start to miss them, I get out a box of pictures and other stuff they have given me, and I feel like they are right next to me."

107 A seventh grade girl lovingly shares, "Because we don't see each other a lot, my mother, stepfather, and I have *Family Day* every Sunday. We cook dinner together, watch movies, etc. This is a memorable time we spend together."

My goal in bringing you all the remarkable things that came *out of the mouth of babes* is to help us to remember that our kids do want us to spend time with them. We can't kid ourselves into thinking otherwise—nor should we.

Talking with Mike Romero

I recently had a heartfelt interview with Mike Romero, whose son, Colorado Army Guard Sgt. 1st Class Daniel Aaron Romero, was killed on April 15, 2002 near Kandahar when a 107mm rocket exploded while he was destroying captured weapons. Aaron was married to Stephanie Wendorf, and the immediate family he kept connected with also included his mom and two sisters. We talked about some of the ways the entire family stayed in touch during Aaron's deployment. Mike was generous and giving with his thoughts. Instead of isolating his ideas into other places in the book, I decided to bring you a summary of what we talked about during the interview.

As we started, Mike talked about how difficult it was to be apart. "You send a strong, capable man off to the military to do a job, but you're still sending your son. Everything you do as a parent must be encouraging and supportive because it's hard on them, too." Mike remembers hearing one soldier remark, "You know what? I'm scared," as he was being deployed.

What were the most effective ways you found to stay in touch?

"Mostly the use of email, and then while stateside, the cell phone and voice mail." This let Aaron keep in touch with his wife. He could call every Sunday, even though Stephanie wouldn't know what time. Email worked best, especially when Aaron was stationed in Germany. Sometimes a commander would have a laptop in the field, and except for high security areas, it could occasionally allow them to link together.

What was the least effective form of communication?

For Mike, it turned out to be regular mail. "The time that it would take, sometimes five weeks, for mail to be sent and received was frustrating." It was particularly difficult for Mike when his family received a letter from Aaron two weeks after his funeral.

But regular mail *is* good for care packages. The soldiers like getting these—and not just for the goodies inside. "It gave the soldiers a chance to share their family with others by sharing the care package. The soldiers had a chance to talk about home."

What did Aaron like best in his care packages?

"Homemade elk or deer jerky."

Could you offer some insight on how to stay connected?

"Connect in whatever form is possible; just remember that it's incredibly important to the soldier in the field to have that link back to wherever home is. When you're overseas in peacetime, it's not as critical. Now, when danger is ever present, the soldiers realize that to make a connection with someone at home is critical to their frame of mind and in a war zone there's always another soldier whose life is dependent upon you. Every time I talked to Aaron, I could tell from his voice how much it meant to him to hear our voices."

Any final thoughts?

"Emails are great when there are pictures attached!"

Mike, thank you.

About Family Services Centers

There are many unique demands imposed on a military family during the course of a military career. These range from frequent relocations and separations, to living with the threat and risk of injury or death. These demands can make it more difficult to fulfill both work and family commitments. This has been particularly hard since the events of September 11, 2001, and the increased activation of Reserve troops. Right now, 48% of active military troops are in National Guard and Reserve units.[4]

Following the abolition of the draft in 1973, the government saw the need for coordinating the military and family lives of its members. This was due to a shift from two-thirds single personnel to almost two-thirds married personnel.[5] Family Service and Support Centers started to emerge to smooth the conflicting demands of the military lifestyle.

By 1993, an annual congressional appropriation of $137 million funded a worldwide network of 370 Family Centers with a combined staff of 3,150 human services professionals. Despite the impacts of downsizing, today the DoD (Department of Defense) retains more than 290 Family Centers around the world...for 670,000 service members with 1.3 million children.[6]

This book could not have been possible without the care and cooperation of representatives and volunteers from military Family Readiness Centers. All branches of the service have a form of this center available to service personnel. They may be called Family Services, Family Readiness, Family Support Centers, or programs under the Chaplain's Office. They describe themselves as "families helping families," and they all do their part to ensure that military members and their families experience the highest possible quality of life.

Military leaders learn early that "if you take care of the people, the people take care of the mission."[7] These Centers use peacetime to build strength, trust, and resources so that they are able to be most effective during activation. Each state operates units and groups that are a vital part of a larger program that continues all the way to the Pentagon.

The military family is also part of a larger family—their military community. The Family Readiness Group establishes a link with this community to help promote awareness. Communication is a major goal for the unit volunteers. They get involved with tasks like developing a telephone tree as a quick system for passing messages to Guard and family members. Other lines of communication can include unit newsletters, questionnaires, volunteer coordination, and an annual conference. To help increase social integration, they network with other local and off-base organizations and civic groups. Maintaining these relationships provides open contact and awareness of the Centers' programs and their professional counterparts. This results in less duplication of services and more collaboration.

Family Readiness Centers are a vital part of helping families get ready for deployment. They can help a family plan ahead and take care of legal, medical, financial, and personal issues. Specifically, a military family can work with their Readiness Center for assistance with referrals and questions. These questions can fall into, but not be limited to, the following issues:

- Personal property
- Estate planning
- Wills and guardianship
- Powers of attorney
- Family problems or difficulties
- Mail
- Benefits and assistance
- Insurance
- Housing and relocation
- Military installation facilities
- Chaplain support
- Alcohol and drug abuse prevention programs
- Spouse employment aid
- Mobilization
- Transition to civilian career
- Family life skills education

You may not be aware of how vital the Family Readiness Centers are. Guidance and support are offered to extended family members (parents, grandparents, etc.) of service men and women. Members of the community sometimes get involved, as well. Many companies or corporations sponsor Reserve units by sending mail and/ or gifts, and doing nice things for the service members' families who remain behind.

Family Service Centers ultimately show us that we ALL have a stake in our military families. The members of the armed forces are out there for us, and we should be a supportive part of bringing them back to a stable and happy family environment.

Resources and Support

National Family Military Association, Inc.
Email: families@nmga.org
The only private national organization designed to identify and resolve issues of concern for military families. Serves all uniformed services.

www.redcross.org
American Red Cross

www.redcross.org/services/afes/
American Red Cross Armed Forces Emergency Services

www.operationuplink.org
Donate a calling card through Operation Uplink.

http://anyservicemember.nave.mil or
http://www.OperationDearAbby.net
Email greetings through Operation Dear Abby.

http://www.defendamerica.mil/nmam/html
Sign a virtual thank you card to military members.

Military relief societies:

http://www.usometrodc.org/care
Donate to "Operation USA Care Package."

http://www.aerhq.org
Army Emergency Relief

http://www.nmcrs.org
Navy/Marine

http://www.afas.org
Air Force Aid Society

http://cgmahq.org
Coast Guard

www.sgtmoms.com
Sgt. Mom's is "Military Life explained by a Military Wife!" It is not an official DoD site or related to any official organization. It's a fun site filled with relevant information and links presented in a clear, navigable site.

www.deploymentlink.osd.mil
DeploymentLINK is maintained by the Office of the Special Assistant to the Under Secretary of Defense for Medical readiness and deployments. It links to National Guard and Reserve web sites.

www.read2kids.org/uniting.htm
The Family Literacy Foundation provides a program for military families to help keep parents and children connected during deployment through reading aloud on videotapes.

www.abanet.org/family/checklist.doc.
A volunteer lawyers group has prepared a Family Member Pre-Deployment Checklist. It is designed for all families and includes record-keeping questions related to medical care, finances, etc.

www.armycommunityservice.org/home.asp
Army Community Service provides real-life solutions for successful Army living.

www.lifelines2000.org/home/htm or
www.lifelines2000.org/services/deployment/index.asp
LIFElines services network is designed primarily for
members of the Marine Corps and the Navy. Offers
downloadable resources (ex: a checklist of things to
remember in the week before departure). What do you
want to know? It's all here for you.

www.defenselink.mil/ra/familyreadiness.html
Resources such as the Family Readiness Toolkit and
Guide to Reserve Family Member Benefits Handbook in
PDF format are available on this site.

www.divorceNet.com
Military divorce, family law and counseling. Source of
articles and information.

www.4MilitaryFamilies.com
Support groups, discounts, travel, housing and
deployment information.

www.mfri.purdue.edu
Military Family Institute is a DoD sponsored research
center with a focus on families.

http://www.dfas.mil/money/garnish/supp-qa.htm
Defense Finance and Accounting Service answers some
FAQ's about child support issues.

www.mfrc.calib.com
Military Family Resource Center is a resource for those
providing services to active duty service members,
reservists, and their families.

www.Groww.com
GroWW is an independent haven for the bereaved developed by the bereaved—OUR PLACE. Message boards and resource listings.

http://Militarywivesandmoms.org/godblessusa.html
A site designed for those who have husbands, sons, or daughters proudly serving our country in the armed forces.

www.Military.com
Connecting you to the benefits of service. It's an amazing site filled with information pertaining to all branches of services. It's always kept current.

http://www.bluestarmothers.org
Designed for mothers who have, or have had children serving in the military. Good information easily arranged.

Volunteer opportunities:

Are you finding yourself a little lonely with some extra time on your hands? Consider volunteering for a worthwhile organization based on your interests. Here are a few sites to start with:

www.adoptaclassroom.org
Connects the community and the classroom. Contribute to the education of young people.

www.beadsforlife.com
Make bead key chains and necklaces that call attention to early detection of breast cancer.

www.Chemocaps.com
This site is for knitters. Donate your time by knitting caps for cancer patients. Comfort their heads and their souls.

http://h4ha.org/snuggles
Hugs for Homeless Animals is a site designed to wrap animals with love by sewing or knitting warm blankets for animals.

www.Projectlinus.org/index.html
Provides love, security, warmth, and comfort to children who are seriously ill or traumatized, through gifts of new/ homemade washable blankets.

http://www.wtv-one.com/kjsb/bataan.html
The Ships Project
Supports American troops at sea and on the ground in Operation Enduring Freedom. Crochet, knit or quilt.

Epilogue

It's been a wonderful journey sharing the ways that families around the world have learned the joy of staying connected.

I'm closing this book with one of the most appropriate emails I have ever received. I believe that it sums up most of what we've been talking about all along. It touched me so much that I have it hanging on the wall in my office. It was a reply to me from my son who is 600 miles away at college, following an email I sent to him advising him of a safety alert for college campuses. Here's what he sent back, and I trust that he won't mind if I share it with you.

Hey Mom, I just wanted to say thank you for that little bit of advice. I will also make sure to tell some of the other people around here. I had no idea that this was a problem. I would have definitely been one to pull over right away for a car with sirens. Thanks for always looking out for me. I know I may get embarrassed sometimes or even upset because you do it so much, but don't listen to me or ever pay attention to that. You always seem to find some way to help me out and I am grateful. You always know what to do. Thanks for looking out for me and loving me as much as you do. Have a wonderful day and I love you. Tell Dad the same for me, please. Talk to you soon. Bryan

I love you, too, Bryan. Goodnight.

In Appreciation

I wish to thank the following people who have shared their "family connection" ideas, and their hearts, to make better families. This project *is* you!

Indy Blaney

Carl Carlson

Zac Chester

Bev Day

SSgt. Eric and Tara Ewing

Anthony D. Fresquez

Major David and Julie-ann Goldstein

Justin Holmes

Julie Hayden

Jeremiah Huerta

Craig Lyons

Rebecca Lyons

Brad Montgomery

Ziggy Rodriquez

Michael Romero

Willow Sterkel

Mark Swenson

LeAnn Thieman

Traci Thomson

Molly Waneka

Lisa White

Permissions

Lines from *The Prophet*, by Kahlil Gibran, are quoted with the permission of Alfred A. Knopf, Inc. Copyright 1923 by Kahlil Gibran, renewed 1951 by Administrator C.T.A. of Kahlil Gibran Estate and Mary G. Gibran.

I'M ALREADY THERE, words and music by Gary Baker, Frank J. Meyers and Richie McDonald. ©2001 Zomba Enterprises Inc., Swear By It Music, Josh/Nick Music and Sony/ATV Songs LLC. All Rights o/b/o Swear By It Music and Josh/Nick Music administered by Zomba Enterprises Inc. All Rights Reserved. Used by permission. WARNER BROS. PUBLICATIONS U.S. INC., Miami, FL 33014.

Zits cartoons permission: ©Zits Partnership. Reprinted with special permission of King Features Syndicate.

Excerpt from *Daily Word*™: reprinted with permission of Unity®, publisher of *Daily Word*.™

Innocence© by Molly Waneka, reprinted with permission of Molly Waneka.

Footnotes

1. Article – "Military Families in the Millennium", from the newsletter entitled *Family Focus on...Military Families* (issue FF13), published by the National Council on Military Relations.

2. Article – "What Society can Learn from the U.S. Military's System of Family Support" by Sondra Albano, Ph.D. in *Family Focus*, March 2002.

3. *Soldier Attitudes: Military Deployments,* U.S. Army Medical Research Unit-Europe, Walter Reed Army Institute of Research, U.S. Army Medical Research and Materiel Command.

4. From *60 Minutes* Newsmagazine report aired on March 16, 2003 on CBS affiliate station KCNC, Denver, Colorado

5. ibid. footnote 2

6. ibid. footnote 2

7. ibid. footnote 2

About the author...

Elaine Dumler is a corporate trainer and speaker who counsels businesses on how their employees and managers can improve their speaking and communication skills. She also advises business people on how they can bring balance to their lives by staying connected with their families.

She achieves this by specializing in workshops that focus on business presentation skills and corporate or entrepreneurial networking— capitalizing on your ability to talk to people. She also helps project teams cut time and money while working together better.

Elaine formed *Frankly Speaking...* to work with people who wish to bring a sense of "craftsmanship" into their business presentations. She presents programs internationally for such organizations as General Electric, Johnson & Johnson, and the U.S. government.

She was a columnist in an international newsletter, and has been a featured guest on both radio and television sharing her knowledge. She is the author of "10 Keys to Comfortable Conversation" and co-author of the book *Marketing for People NOT in Marketing.*

She's married to a middle school math teacher and has a son at Kansas University majoring in Engineering. She loves to quilt, hates to cook, and travels about a third of her time for business. She may be contacted at Elaine@ElaineDumler.com.

Also by Elaine Dumler

♥ ...Booklet: 10 Keys to Comfortable Conversation

♥ ... Book: Marketing for People NOT in Marketing—
How Everyone Can Build Customer Relationships

♥ ... "In the Arms of an Angel"—Story in *Chicken Soup for the Nurse's Soul*

♥ ... BusinessNotes©—professional series: An easy way to keep in touch and give support to business friends and customers. (Set of 10 different notecards.)

♥ ... BusinessNotes©—referral series: A professional way to keep in touch and say thank you to business friends and customers. (Set of 10 notecards.)

Order Form

- FAX ORDERS   303-430-7679
- TELEPHONE ORDERS   Call Toll Free: 1-866-780-0460
- ONLINE ORDERS   www.ImAlreadyHome.com
- POSTAL ORDERS   Frankly Speaking
                      6460 W. 98th Court
                      Westminster, CO 80021

- TELEPHONE   303-430-0592

Please send me the following:

_____ Book(s) - *I'm Already Home*
Keeping Your Family Close when You're on TDY ...... $11.95 ea.

_____ Information on how to **sponsor books** into military
families or Centers **at special pricing**

_____ Information on how to be a part of **distributing
sponsored books**

_____ Book(s) - *Marketing for People NOT
in Marketing* .... $14.95 ea.

Company Name _____

Name _____

Address _____

City _____ State _____ Zip _____

Telephone (_____) _____

Email _____

SALES TAX
Please add 4% for books shipped to Colorado address.

SHIPPING
$2.00 for the first book and $1.00 for each additional book.

Total Payment $ _____

_____ Check   _____ Credit Card: _____Visa   _____ MasterCard

Card Number _____ Exp. ____ / ____

Signature _____

CALL TOLL FREE AND ORDER NOW!
1-866-780-0460